WHO'S LOOKING AT MY THIGHS, ANYWAY?

LAURA WEINTRAUB STELLINO

Copyright © 2022 Laura Weintraub Stellino.

All Rights Reserved. This book contains material protected under International and Federal Copyright Laws and Treaties. Any unauthorized reprint or use of this material is prohibited. No part of this book may be reproduced or transmitted in any form or by any means, electronic or mechanical, including photocopying, recording, or by any information storage and retrieval system without express written permission from the author/publisher.

ISBN: 978-1-7374312-2-0 paperback
ISBN: 978-1-7374312-3-7 ebook

CONTENTS

Preface	v
Chapter One: The Emptiness Inside	1
Chapter Two: A Very Public Shaming	5
Chapter Three: Maybe Baby	8
Chapter Four: Selfish Scares	14
Chapter Five: It Isn't Easy, Mama	18
Chapter Six: Letting Go	23
Chapter Seven: From Nobody to Somebody	31
Chapter Eight: Who Am I Now	36
Chapter Nine: Anxiety and Antidepressants	41
Chapter Ten: Goodbye Dad	46
Chapter Eleven: My Biggest Critic	49
Chapter Twelve: Breaking Free	55
Chapter Thirteen: Rising Above	59

PREFACE

There comes a point in most people's lives at which they make the conscious decision to live more openly, as their true, authentic self. After staring at years full of raw journals and having a burning desire to drop my bullshit facade, I created this book. What is written between these covers is my story, but if you have ever found yourself comforted by hearing a relatable journey of another, then I hope these words will assure you that you are not alone.

CHAPTER ONE
THE EMPTINESS INSIDE

Others looked at me and assumed my life was perfect. The husband, the kids, the house… but what they didn't see, is what my experience was like inside. The emptiness, the disgust, the self-hatred.

People think I'm crazy when I tell them I've always felt like a huge failure. They are impressed by my previous careers and the many things I have experienced, but in *my* mind, I never had anything to show for it. This is something I have struggled with for most of my adult life.

I was convinced that money equaled success. Period. I have since learned that idea is bullshit because no matter how much money I made; it didn't make a dent in my inner worth. My opinion of myself stayed in the gutter for years.

I used to wonder how other people succeeded at life. What brought them happiness and joy? How did they always see the glass half-full? What did they do differently and why wasn't I able to do the same? I believe we are all born with an immeasurable amount of optimism and positivity, but holding onto it is another story for some. My unstable upbringing is what seemed to chisel away at my inner value. As the years went on, I went from being whole to something that needed to be fixed.

When my kids were born, I was determined to do whatever I could to raise positive, emotionally balanced individuals. I wanted them to have the self-confidence I lacked.

One thing I planned to do was minimize my use of the word "no" with my children. I imagined that responding in an encouraging way with more "yeses" would result in bringing up more positive kids. Reflecting back, this theory is now quite laughable to me, because I feel like most days "NO" is the only word in my vocabulary. What about my own childhood? I wonder if I was told "no" often? Although, as an only child, I probably didn't get into quite as much trouble as the tag-teaming toddlers I'm raising.

My parents divorced when I was two years old. I lived with my mom full time and was forced to visit my dad and new stepfamily every other weekend. I say forced because the visits were truly awful and contributed heavily to my lack of self-worth. I don't have many memories of those days, but what I do recall very clearly is feeling unsafe in my surroundings and having a dad who never stood up for me. It wasn't like I was blatantly abused, but the feelings of not being loved or wanted were very apparent. At my dad's house, my stepsiblings were catered to and cared for, while I was treated like Cinderella — before she went to the ball. I begged endlessly for my father's attention, but my longing for him was unacknowledged.

Eventually, my mom recognized how distressing and anxiety-provoking these weekend visits were for me, which led her to pursue and win full custody. Even then, with limited visitation, I still found myself yearning for my dad's unattainable attention. This went on for nearly two decades until I finally surrendered and chose to accept my father and his family just as they were. I gave up my expectations, set aside my feelings of pain and abandonment, and made the choice to accept my dad for who he was. This shift is what allowed us to finally have somewhat of a father-daughter relationship before it was too late, as he died unexpectedly soon thereafter.

My dad's flawed parenting took a big toll on my personal life and subsequently my relationships with men. I always sought the hard-to-get type; the bad boys, the assholes, and the ones who left me feeling never quite good enough — just like I felt with my dad. It was a fucked-up way of thinking. I spent so much of my life seeking attention and approval from the opposite sex. It was exhausting. Thanks, dad.

If I gained anything from my ongoing battle for attention, it was persistence, and I applied it full-force to something I loved to do: roller-skate. Skating became my life. I diligently practiced every day, and spent more time at our local skating rink than I did at home.

Figure skating was my first competitive sport, and it held my interest for years until I was introduced to roller hockey. I fell in love with hockey. Being one of the only females in the local league gave me plenty of male attention in a healthy way, and I loved being in the spotlight. It was as though I was born to be just that.

I'll admit, I still catch myself searching for that feeling of recognition, but it's different now. I'm different now. I am actually the epitome of an introvert, so much so, that it is often daunting. I usually dread going out in public — even just to the mailbox or grocery store. I don't want anyone to notice me, yet part of me also dislikes being unnoticed.

My avoidance of people and preference for "alone time" worked just fine before I became a parent. I don't want my extroverted kids to feel isolated as a result of my extreme shyness, so I consciously make an effort to be more outgoing. I want their childhood to be carefree and filled with fun and exploration. Hopefully, they are getting enough of that.

CHAPTER TWO
A VERY PUBLIC SHAMING

Embarrassment has been a recurring theme throughout my life. Have you ever been so embarrassed, humiliated, or publicly shamed that you felt like you wanted to die? Have you ever felt like the whole world was against you? I have, and it was something I thought I would never recover from. If you have ever gone through a very public shaming, you might have an idea of what I'm talking about.

I've always enjoyed poking fun at life and I found it was easier to hide behind my sense of humor than let anyone know what was really going on inside. Several years ago, I created satirical YouTube videos called "Cupholder Commentary." Although they were mainly for my own entertainment, I loved the comments from those who shared my same sense of humor. Since feeling loved and accepted was something I longed for most of my life, the responses to my videos helped fulfill that need. It was similar to the sense of fulfillment that skating professional roller derby provided two decades earlier. More about that later.

Most of my YouTube skits were self-deprecating and viewers seemed to enjoy them. I produced a new video every week and people would thank me for making them laugh. I loved it! Until the dreadful day one of my commentaries didn't go over as planned. Unbeknownst to me at the time, making a video about cyclists was going to be my last.

Ignorance isn't always bliss, and my lack of awareness about a very real issue riders face bit me in the ass. My video included sarcastic comments about running over cyclists and a photo I found on the web depicting a horrific cycling accident. I had no idea the image I used was real and that the hatred against cyclists is an ongoing challenge they battle. The irony of it is that I never really had anything against cyclists.

I was working as a reserve police officer when this took place, and I found myself forced into a very sudden and embarrassing resignation as a result of the whole ordeal. I get it. It didn't look good on the department's behalf to continue to employ me after I caused such a national "misunderstanding." When I say national, I mean Entertainment fucking Tonight came to my house to interview me about it.

Sorry about all of the "fucks" — it has always been a favorite word of mine.

Following my very public faux pas, I received thousands of threats from across the globe through all means of communication: social media, email, and my cell phone. This went on for what seemed like an endless amount of time. Even my husband's job was jeopardized in the uproar. Because many of these threats were death threats, I was afraid to leave my house unarmed. When I did go out, I was just as terrified to return home. I hung curtains in every bare window and covered my face at the grocery store. This was one of the hardest times in my life and I didn't think it was ever going to end. I was going to be publicly shamed and hated for all of eternity.

There was literally nothing I could do about this unanticipated situation. How was I going to stop this war against me? An apology to the masses was needed, and as much as I wanted to bury my head forever, I chose to film a follow-up video to do just that. The new video showed the *real* me, not the person I pretended to be in my weekly skits.

It was my hope that if people could see who I really was, they would know that I never had the intention of causing harm to anyone. It was a huge relief when my public apology seemed to smooth things over — but not with the police department. I will always remember the day I turned in my department-issued badge and gun. I worked so hard for those and I was always honored to have held that position. My pride was crushed, and my heart was broken.

CHAPTER THREE
MAYBE BABY

For as long as I can remember, I loved everything about police work. When I lost my position, it hit hard. I had spent years applying and testing with nearly every department in California, and was turned down by every single one of them. The reason? Because I am too fucking honest. I kid you not — that's the goddamned truth, and it doesn't make any sense.

The most important part of the hiring process is the detailed background application. Prior to filling out any paperwork, applicants are warned about withholding information. If they do, they will immediately forfeit their opportunity for a position within that department, and will also not be eligible for hire by any other agency. Following those intimidating instructions, I disclosed every detail of my past, including the time I flashed my boobs on a boat in Lake Tahoe six years prior. No one would have *ever* found out about it, so I was sure my honesty would be appreciated. I mean after all, who hasn't done a thing or two like that in their twenties? Well, apparently, the key to getting hired is lying — and I am a shitty, awful liar.

I was so turned off by all of the bullshit, yet still, I wanted in. I don't like to give up on things. Actually, I'm not sure if I've ever really given up, or surrendered to anything. By now the only shot I had at getting into a department would be by enrolling myself into the reserve police academy — but even that wouldn't come with the assurance of being employed upon completion.

My idea was to get hired as a reserve officer, which would hopefully open a door to a full-time position. I made it as far as the reserve part, and then my viral video had other plans for me. Or maybe it was God with the bigger plan, perfectly orchestrated on my behalf, through intense public humiliation. They say if it wasn't meant to be, it's only because there is something better out there for you.

Law enforcement was a life-long passion that began in grammar school with the Drug Abuse Resistance Education program. In my early teens, I became a dedicated Sheriff's Explorer, attended every meeting and made my way through the ranks. When I aged out of the program, becoming a police officer was the natural next step. How did I not notice the signs that perhaps this was not the right path for me? It started with the overwhelming number of rejections. Then there was the time I was on my way home from the shooting range and was rear-ended on the freeway. The accident led to tremendous chronic pain that made it nearly impossible to wear my duty belt, yet I persevered. Was there really something better out there for me?

One of the most difficult aspects of all of this was my loss of identity, but that was about to change. I was about thirty-six at the time and my biological clock had been ticking for a while; even though I couldn't fully picture myself as a mom. My husband, Jason, and I had been trying for over a year to get pregnant with no success. Jay always wanted to have kids, but I wasn't quite sure if motherhood was for me. I never had the dream I imagined most girls had growing up; the idea of a house with a white-picket fence, handsome husband, babies running around, playing dress-up, planting in the garden and cooking elaborate meals. To be honest, I just didn't feel like the mothering type. As in; not nurturing, too self-centered — you get the picture. But I was also closer to forty than thirty, and wasn't getting any younger.

I wondered what life would be like in ten, twenty, thirty years without kids. Would I have regret? What would it be like *with* kids? Would I have regret? Which one would likely lead to less regret? My worry was that I would miss out on something important.

Naively, I thought getting pregnant would be easy but that wasn't my experience. It took nearly two years. I will never forget the unsettling feelings every month that came with peeing on a stick; that nervousness while waiting for my timer to buzz and the nauseating pit in my stomach. You would think I would have gotten used to it, having seen so many failed tests before — but each time felt as disappointing as the first.

It was in the Fall of 2014 and the day before we were scheduled to leave on our traditional family Thanksgiving trip, when I half-heartedly took another pregnancy test. "I'M PREGNANT!!" I screamed from the bathroom after my tenth glance at that cheap piece of plastic. It finally happened! The next evening, Jason and I surprised my family with an impromptu, make-shift photo book that included years of past Thanksgivings, and ended with a picture of my "positive" pregnancy test. That was a memorable moment. My poor mom, I think she assumed she would never be known as "grandma." Actually, she still isn't, as our kids lovingly refer to her as their "matae." Yes, just like it's spelled and I don't have a clue where it came from.

Our weekend away came and went, and soon after, I began seeing an obstetrician for routine ultrasounds. We got to the point when it was time for genetic testing, which would reveal the baby's gender. I was so excited about this, and deep down, even though I would always say I just wanted a healthy baby, I really wanted a boy. I waited impatiently for days to hear from the doctor with my test results, but instead, the call I received had some very unexpected news: I was a carrier of cystic fibrosis. My world stopped and my mind went blank. "*What is cystic fibrosis?*" I thought in that paralyzing moment. I had heard of it, but what exactly did it mean to be a carrier? Was our baby carrying it too? If so, then what? Questions began flooding through my mind at an incomprehensible rate. Now what?? I jumped on Google and freaked the fuck out. The internet has a special way of doing that. The next step was for Jason to be tested. If both of us carried the gene, then there was a one in four chance that our baby would have CF. The numbers got a little better when I learned that Jason would have only a one in twenty-seven percent chance of being a carrier. As much as I love to gamble, these odds didn't make me feel optimistic.

Jay had his blood drawn the next day and then came the unbearable process of waiting. I fucking hate waiting. I hate waiting in lines, I hate waiting for food, I hate waiting for anything and this was just the worst. I spent the next week being as mindful as I could with my thinking, trying not to let worry get the best of me. I knew all of my speculations were fear-driven, and it is best to set those kinds of thoughts aside whenever possible. *Just keep refocusing, just keep refocusing.* It was like a running mantra to myself in an effort to keep my mind out of worry and as far away as possible from the worst-case scenario.

The days slowly crept along, and then, finally; the doctor's office called. They were calling to tell us what our baby's gender was, not to give us the test results I had been painfully waiting for. As much as I wanted to know *what* we were expecting, I had to tell the receptionist to withhold that information until I knew the outcome of Jason's blood work. Knowing the gender just seemed so insignificant in that anxious, unnerving moment. "Oh!" she said. "I think we got those results back, too — hang on while I go check." *Could she have been any more nonchalant with such important information??* It seemed like the longest thirty seconds of my life until she came back on the line and let me know that Jason was **not** a carrier! "Would you like to know the gender now?" she quickly asked. *Wait, wait, wait*! I had to catch my breath before she could go on, and when I did, she told me we were going to have a baby boy! Oh my God! A BOY! I jumped up and down, screaming with excitement at the news!

CHAPTER FOUR
SELFISH SCARES

The next twenty weeks went by uneventfully, which is favorable when you are referring to a pregnancy. The only concerning thing at this point was that our baby was still in a breech position, but I was assured many times by both the doctor *and* Google, that more often than not, a baby will turn head down in the last few weeks of gestation. To me, the worrisome part of my breech boy was the possibility of needing a caesarean delivery. Not only am I terrified of surgery, from everything I had read, a C-section would surely ruin my body — a body I had worked so hard at shaping for more than two decades.

Although I've never felt completely satisfied with my physique, I was sure this way of birthing our baby would just destroy it. That scar, the flap of skin that would hang over the top — I just couldn't go there — so I did what I do best, and turned to Google for support. How could I get this baby to flip around? Well, I spent the next seventeen weeks trying to figure it out. Positioning myself upside down, standing on my head, placing a flashlight at the base of my belly in an attempt to "lure" his head downwards and finally, moxibustion, a type of Chinese medicine that involves burning moxa close to the skin at an acupuncture point on the little toe. You name it — I did it — and not a damn thing worked. I'd like you to know that my son is now five and still a stubborn little shit a lot of the time.

There was one last thing to try in hopes of getting this baby to flip, and that was to attempt an external cephalic version (ECV). Yikes! I had come across videos of the procedure in my Google searches, but didn't think I'd ever have to go that far to get this boy's head turned down. My doctor let me know that I was an ideal candidate for the procedure (long torso coupled with a small baby), and I decided it was the next best step to take — or so I thought at the time. ECV is where a doctor or chiropractor physically tries to manipulate a breech baby into a head-down position. Typically, ECV's are performed in a hospital after thirty-seven weeks gestation. There is a very small possibility of the procedure causing distress to the baby, and that distress would lead to an emergency C-section.

As awful as it sounded, there was only a four percent chance of that happening. One week later, we headed to the hospital for the big attempt. I, of course, didn't pack a bag, because I knew we would be headed home just an hour or so later. Well, that didn't exactly happen. Not even close.

I lay nervously and cold on a gurney in my hospital gown, waiting for the doctor to come in. He threw me a curve ball when he recommended that I have an epidural for the procedure. Okay, you're talking to someone who doesn't even like to take an Advil, let alone something that would cause her lower body to go numb! And this is suggested why? I inquired. From everything I had read, the procedure is not supposed to be that painful. "Well," he said, "you can go without, but if for any reason we need to do an emergency C-section, we will be forced to knock you out in order to save the baby, and you won't see your newborn for quite some time afterward." Well shit, numb me up, Doc. I had the epidural just before being transferred to the operating room table, where I was surrounded by a bunch of new faces. Doctors, nurses, assistants, all gathered around, doing their various jobs — one of which was to ultrasound my belly so they were able to keep an eye on my boy throughout the procedure.

After a good amount of forceful pushing and prodding on my abdomen, my doctor suddenly stopped and said (very calmly, in retrospect) that the baby's heartbeat had dropped a little and they needed to wait for it to recover before making any further attempts. I was enveloped in fear as I lay there waiting, but those moments paled in comparison to what happened next. ***"CODE BLUE! We have an emergency C-section — all personnel to the OR"*** or something like that, was all I heard as I watched everyone around me scatter, putting on surgical scrubs and gathering the materials needed to cut me open. The setting around me erupted into utter chaos and I was terrified. Our son's heart rate was dropping and he needed out NOW! I don't think I had ever experienced that level of icy terror before. I mean, I was supposed to be on my way back home long ago — where I would wait out the final few weeks of my pregnancy.

Then just as suddenly as the chaos had begun, it was called off. The demeanor in the room shifted, and the hurried pace returned to normal. What the fuck just happened?! The doctor explained that the baby's heart rate had picked back up and that he was going to be just fine. The ECV failed, but that was the least of my concerns. I was wheeled back to my hospital room where I remained numb from the epidural, exhausted from all of my anxiety, and feeling like such a selfish asshole for putting our unborn child though something SO distressing — just so that I could increase my chances of having him vaginally. I guess you could say that my first lesson in selflessness and parenting hit hard. He could still flip, Dr. Google told me, but I didn't hold my breath.

CHAPTER FIVE
IT ISN'T EASY, MAMA

I scheduled a C-section for July 28th, 2015. Twenty-eight has always been a special number in our family. Jason's mom was born on the 28th of October, and he has always worn that number on his hockey jersey in her honor. I never had the chance to know Kari, as she lost her battle with cancer about three years before I met Jason, but I am convinced she must have been a very special woman. I have felt her presence several times over the years; the most noticeable occasion took place while I was washing a beautiful crystal vase that once belonged to her. Although it isn't often, I have moments where I see beyond what appears to be here. This started at a young age, when I would see apparitions roaming about in my childhood home — but now I'm usually too knee-deep in kids to even notice.

The days leading up to my C-section overflowed with mixed emotions. I wanted more than anything to be excited. After all, if you count the time spent trying to conceive this little bundle, I had been waiting more than two years to meet him. That late July morning finally arrived and I was *petrified*. To top it off, I had to have an empty stomach, which translated to no coffee. If you know me at all, you know that's not good.

It was 4:30 a.m. when we headed to the hospital for check-in and prep, stopping only to pick up some ice for our cooler at the corner gas station. No, it wasn't for post-birth celebration libations — it was for my placenta. I made prior arrangements to have it encapsulated, as I had heard that ingesting the placenta could be beneficial in the early postpartum period. I didn't really have anything to compare it to, as this was definitely my first rodeo, but what I am certain of is that it didn't help me to breastfeed as I had so hoped it would. Placenta consumption is said to increase milk production, but I was as dry as the Sahara, despite my best efforts.

The end of my short-lived breastfeeding journey crushed my heart; I felt like a complete failure. The health nut, tree-hugging type of mama I sometimes feel like inside wanted to make sure my baby had the best of everything from the start, and from what I knew — or thought I knew — that meant he would consume only breast milk. And please, mamas who breast-fed, I am not slamming you in the slightest, it's just that there are always a select few who seem to have a knack for making anyone who isn't breast feeding feel like worthless garbage. According to them, it was as though I were intentionally poisoning my child by giving him formula. *So, what you're telling me, is that he would be better off starving due to my lack of production than drinking a man-made milk?* Don't even get me started on all of the things I did in a desperate attempt to get my milk flowing. Being a new mom is hard enough. Being a new mom who feels judged and criticized by another mom, just flat-out freaking sucks. If you've been there, you know what I am talking about.

Those first few months with a new baby are challenging. I had huge expectations of myself and set ridiculous, idealized standards I thought I needed to adhere to. Currently, there is even more pressure on new moms — thanks to social media. I felt like I had to have my shit together through it all. Perfect hair, fit body, spotless house, perfectly dressed kids — even my dog had to look great in my photos. Maybe this is why my Instagram account hasn't been active since my first baby shower, which is probably the last time I looked halfway decent. I wish I were joking.

As the months went by, I discovered just how demanding motherhood can be. Caring for one baby was much harder than I imagined, so I was surprised when the desire arose a have another. Here I was struggling to stay balanced with one child, and along came our daughter, Lexi Jo, affectionately known as *Birdie*. Her nickname came from her twenty-two-month-old brother, Landon, who couldn't quite say the word "baby." This girl has been a spitfire since birth.

I thought I wanted a second boy and I spent a good amount of time in tears following our gender reveal. I just didn't feel like I had what it would take to be a good role model to a daughter. I've always been more of a tomboy, and I have even joked about myself feeling like a man trapped in a woman's body. I have always related better to men and admired their laid-back approach to life. I thought it would be a less demanding and easier way to live.

My mom has joked that my having a girl would be payback for some of the things I did in my youth. It would take a lot for my daughter to even touch the amount of torment I put my mom through. People don't believe me when I tell them how difficult I was as a child. I think most of my challenging behavior was a direct result of what I experienced in my early years with my dad — and it was my poor mom who endured the brunt of it. I remember feeling wrought with depression and anxiety throughout my preteen and teen years. One particular episode was so bad that my mom flew home from her father's deathbed in Florida, fearing I might end my life if she didn't return immediately.

Our daughter, Lexi, is now two-years-old, and between her and her brother, I think I have reached a whole new level of mom-crazy. I don't know what else to call it, probably because it's not really talked about.

How often do you hear another mother admit she's really struggling? It's a taboo subject. As a new mom, I was afraid there was something wrong with me if my life didn't appear perfect; and yet what I felt inside was the complete opposite. I thought if I let down my guard, I would risk being seen as a failure. I think being able to talk about the challenges of motherhood should be normalized instead of labeled. I can't begin to tell you how many mothers of older kids would tell me to, "Enjoy every moment" or "Enjoy every moment because it goes so fast." I understand. I know it goes by quickly. But when you are in the thick of it, these are the last things you want to hear. There were times I felt I was doing everything wrong; so when someone would tell me to just "enjoy," it wasn't helpful and it brought on the guilt. This was all so much simpler when the only "children" I had in my life had four legs, like my Heart Dog, Titan.

CHAPTER SIX
LETTING GO

A Heart Dog is a once-in-a-lifetime, soulmate dog, and mine came in the form of a 160-pound merlequin-colored Great Dane. There are two things I have always been fond of — oversized trucks and giant dogs. Titan was a perfect match.

I had always envisioned having a male, harlequin, Great Dane with cropped ears, so when my mom and I went to meet Titan, he really didn't fit my expectations. He was male, but the wrong color and his big, goofy ears flopped hopelessly all over the place. Surely, he was perfect — just not for me — as I had a different idea of perfection in mind. I returned home and went on with life, waiting for another breeder to announce they had puppies for sale.

Several days passed and my mom said she just couldn't stop thinking about Titan. I should mention that mom has always had excellent intuition, so when she can't get something out of her mind, I pay attention.

The very next day we returned to the breeder, and it didn't take long for me to fall completely in love. Titan seemed to grow bigger by the hour, and within a few short months I bought a new vehicle to accommodate his rapidly growing size. Titan, or Ty, as I often referred to him, was my constant companion and went everywhere with me. Looking back, he had become an unexpected source of emotional support. I felt more confident when he was around; which helped me overcome some of the challenges that came with being an introvert. Titan also attracted quite a bit of male attention — which, as an extremely shy, single female, provided effortless means into the dating world.

Titan had always had a funny, "wobbly" gait. I thought it was just part of his goofy personality and I didn't give it much thought until I returned home from a weekend away. My world was rocked when I picked up Titan at my mom's house. As I approached the driveway, Titan ran up to greet me. He looked like he was drunk, practically falling over with every step. I knew something was terribly wrong. The veterinarian managed to squeeze Titan into his schedule the following morning. This was when I learned about Wobblers Disease; a progressive decline of a dog's mobility due to compression of their spinal cord. There isn't much that can be done to cure it, so you do your best to manage the inflammation and pain, and hope the progression slows. Watching your dog become slowly paralyzed is heartbreaking.

I researched every possible option as if it were my full-time job, and came across a veterinarian in Indiana, who is well known in the Great Dane world. Dr. Terry Durkes is recognized for his gold-bead implant therapy; an outpatient procedure yielding excellent reviews. After a phone consultation with him, I believed this would offer the best possible outcome for Titan. The following week, my mom, Titan, and I packed up my Honda Element and drove from California to the Midwest for surgery. *Did I mention this was in the dead of winter?* The Element was a second car I had purchased in order to accommodate Titan's declining physical condition, but I was willing to do anything for this dog.

Gold-bead surgery is entirely different from the more common, spine-fusing attempt to halt the progression of the disease. The recovery from traditional spinal surgery is long, difficult, and doesn't guarantee improvement. The gold-bead method was a more favorable option. It was low risk, comfortable, and required hardly any recovery time.

During the procedure, only mild sedation is needed while tiny beads are placed under the skin along the cervical spine. The gold beads continuously stimulate acupressure points, helping to stabilize the spine and reduce the inflammation.

This was our first of two trips to Indiana for the same procedure. Titan had great results the first time, until a few months later when he attempted to go after a deliveryman at our front door. Titan charged through a window as that poor, terrified man was leaving a package. Shattering the glass reinjured his neck, and Dr. Durkes believed that a second round of gold beads would likely be just as helpful as the first. This was well before I had any two-legged kids, so yes; I drove from California back to Indiana to repeat the procedure. After all, Titan *was* my child. He was my world.

The second surgery didn't help as much as I had hoped and I gut-wrenchingly watched as Titan continued to decline. I did everything I could to stop the progression of the disease; I couldn't imagine my life without this dog. Stem-cell therapy was the next step and it was one I would later regret. The procedure didn't go at all the way it had been described to me. It was supposed to be a very minor operation, with just a tiny incision on his belly where the surgeon would draw the cells — a quick, outpatient thing. That wasn't the case, and Titan was cut from his chest to his penis. His recovery was agonizing. It was just too much for his big, beautiful body and I have always wondered if that set him back, instead of offering what I had hoped would be his big turnaround.

Titan continued to decline rapidly. We managed his pain with plenty of narcotics and supplements but I was always worried that his fragile limbs would catch a corner wrong, or trip over a threshold, or do something that would injure him and force me into a rushed good-bye. The thought of that was unbearable and I knew deep down, as hideous as it was to think about, it was getting close to the time to set him free. As much as I thought I wouldn't be able to live without Titan, I also knew that I wouldn't be able to live with myself if I didn't let him go with dignity.

I remember his last day as if it were yesterday. There was such a feeling of not knowing what to do with myself as I waited for the vet to arrive. She wasn't scheduled until 2:30 p.m., and I just didn't know how to "be." *Do I spend every waking second lying next to him? Do I go take care of the dog I was scheduled to walk that day?* (I had started a dog-walking business for large and giant breeds about a year prior.) *At what time should I give him all of his favorite foods?* I didn't want to start too early and risk giving him a bellyache — but I wanted to make sure he had the very best last day. *Last day.* That's still hard to say, almost six years later. I remember going to the grocery store that morning, and buying all of his favorites: steak, mac n' cheese and ice cream. I was in a trance-like state, just going through the motions, completely numb inside. The store clerk smiled, handed me my change, and told me to have a wonderful day. I remember getting back into the car and being so angry! *If only he knew*, I thought, as I sobbed the entire ride home. The rest of the afternoon is a little bit of a blur, but as 2:30 p.m.

grew closer, so did my deep, aching sorrow. *How will I ever go through with this?* How will I make this decision in the final moment and not change my mind? How will I let my very best friend slip away forever, and know it is because of my decision, that he will be leaving?

Titan's bed was a queen-sized mattress on our living room floor that he and I shared every night for the last two years of his life. He often needed help getting up to go outside, and I feared that he might struggle in the middle of the night if I weren't there to assist. I remember lying there that last afternoon, holding his paws, my face buried in his, his breaths becoming shallower and hearing the eventual, empathetic words of his vet: ***"He's gone, Laura."*** And then it was done. He was gone. And a part of me was, too.

Somehow, I lived through it. Somehow, the memories slowly shifted from being able to only recall those final-heart shattering moments, to remembering all the joy Titan brought into my life. Saying goodbye fucking sucks.

Last year it was time to say good-bye to my Jessie Girl in the same gut-wrenching way. The pain was different this time. Perhaps it was because I now had two, two-legged kids that I needed to keep myself together for — but it still sucked. Jessie was with me for nearly a decade. She showed up in my life unexpectedly when someone posted a photo of her on my Facebook timeline. At first glance I thought it was Titan, but it was actually a beautiful, female rescue who was available for adoption — and I had to meet her.

Owning two Great Danes at the same time was a little overwhelming. It reminds me of when you go from having one child to two. It isn't double the work, it's more like quadrupled, and even that feels like an understatement. By the way, moms with more than two kids, I don't know how you manage.

Jessie fought a lengthy battle with liver disease and cancer; yet still somehow made it to eleven. When it was eventually time to let her go, it hit hard in more ways than just the good-bye. She was my last living connection to Titan, and losing her felt like the closing of a book I wasn't ready to put down.

I was pregnant with my first-born when I really began to notice Jessie's decline. It was becoming obvious that she may not be with us for too much longer and I couldn't imagine my life without the companionship of a dog. The thought of dealing with a puppy after having a newborn sounded like it would be a lot of work, so we brought home another Dane before my due date; with the intention of having him trained by the time the baby arrived. Have I mentioned that Danes aren't the sharpest tools in the shed?

"Finn" is a good boy, but the combination of a giant dog and young children is a lot to manage —especially when those kids were itty-bitty and I was constantly worried about them being stepped on, pushed over or hit with a bear-sized paw. Those concerns have lessened over the years, but Finn still manages to make them cry when he steals their snacks or tears apart one of their treasured toys. The damn dog is nearly six and still not trained. Asshole.

CHAPTER SEVEN
FROM NOBODY TO SOMEBODY

Losing Titan and Jessie left an indescribable emptiness in my heart. It was reminiscent of the loss I felt when I learned that RollerJam, a TV show I performed in, was coming to an end. Playing professional roller derby on a nationally syndicated network isn't generally where your skating passion takes you, and honestly, prior to the show's audition, I didn't even know what roller derby was. The only reason I considered trying out was because my hockey teammate told me about it and she really wanted a friend to go with her. I was recently on a "break" from Mark (the love of my life at the time), and figured I didn't have anything to lose. Meaning I was so down in the dumps, that this might have been the pick-me-up that I needed — if I did indeed end up making the team. But really, what were my chances?

I made the two hour trek to a skating rink in Orange County for my audition. After skating a few laps, and answering some questions on camera, I was on my way back home. It felt uneventful so I was shocked when I heard from a producer the next day. He said I was great on camera and acknowledged my skating ability. I couldn't believe I was being invited to Universal Studios in Orlando to film.

At the time, I was eighteen and preparing for my finals at the local college. Feeling lost after my recent break-up, I thought, *why not?* I was stunned when I heard what my starting pay would be — *I'd be making how much to roller skate?!* In my mind, money had always equaled success, which meant for the first time, I would feel worthy; I would finally feel as though I was "enough." Little did I know, this would begin my painful, emotional journey toward another loss.

My mom and I were flown to Florida for a few days so we could see the sound stage at Universal, meet the other skaters, sign contracts and find a place for me to live. This was going to be the first time I would be living on my own. Some teens travel across the states to attend college, others go to play roller derby.

I had enrolled in college just after high school and was there for just a few semesters before I left for the derby. From the moment I arrived in my new hometown of Orlando, life changed dramatically.

Getting my hair and make-up done, tanning, wearing fake nails; these things were all so new to me. Imagine what it was like to go from feeling like an unpopular, unattractive tomboy for most of my life, to a celebrity in the world of sports entertainment. Fans from around the globe sent flowers, gifts, and letters professing their love. I wish I had enjoyed it more in the moment. Instead, I spent much of my time in Florida alone, crying over my failed relationship with Mark. I would have traded my glamorous new life for one more chance with him. At least that's how I felt then. Thankfully that didn't happen, because how often do you get a chance to play roller derby on television?

Derby life was very competitive, especially among the women. Everyone was always trying to get a bigger part, a longer interview, and wear a sexier uniform. From the beginning, I was fortunate to be written into the scripts frequently — meaning I was a featured player. Yes, it was all scripted. I hope I didn't just crush your spirit.

I began my RollerJam career as one of the three "Showgirls" on the Nevada Hot Dice team. One of the other showgirls was a competitive figure-model; she introduced me to new ways of caring for my body. I learned how to eat in order to look my best in our little spandex uniforms. It wasn't long before I started to notice positive changes in my body, and I was sure that the next time I'd see Mark, he wouldn't be able to resist the new me. Even with all the new male attention I was getting, all I wanted was *him*.

This was a tremendously painful and confusing time in my life. How was I good enough for all these people who didn't even know me, while never being enough for the only one who mattered? *Talk about a mind fuck.* I continued to skate roller derby for the next few years, and had some great experiences along the way. About six months into my new career, I started dating someone from another team, and it was the first time I felt like I was moving on from Mark.

My new man was a little older than I was, very attractive, and a lot of fun. Our commonality of professional skating brought us together, but we had similar interests outside of the derby world, too. He had that bad-boy vibe I loved, and at times seemed a tad distant, which foolishly only made me want him more. After being together for some time, I inquired about our seriousness as a couple. I suppose it was his intention I was curious about, as I, of course, knew where I stood. Shortly after that uneventful conversation, he grew more and more unavailable and I soon found out he had a wife back in his hometown in Wisconsin. I was devastated. At least it wasn't over Mark this time — but in a way it was worse, as I still had to face this guy at our daily practices and games.

I survived the rest of the season and then it was break time for the show. Most skaters returned home for the brief time off. I chose to stay in Florida because in my free time I played for a professional roller hockey team and wanted to finish out the season. I waited for the call to let me know it was time to resume filming, but sadly, the phone never rang. Instead, I received a letter: *The show had been cancelled.*

CHAPTER EIGHT
WHO AM I NOW

No more Roller Derby? No more fans? Admiration? Paychecks? No more hair and makeup and sparkles and uniforms and bright lights? No more Showgirls, Pussycat (my last season's character), no more interviews and viewing parties? And definitely no more chances to rekindle my roller derby romance. *Who am I if I am not a professional skater?* This was the question that plagued me for years as I tried my hand at a million other things. *I really did spend the next half decade trying to answer it.* I became a personal trainer, a nutrition coach, an esthetician, a reserve police officer, and a lingerie model. Pursued an acting career, had my own (very) short-lived local television show, launched a vending business, worked for a construction contractor, started a dog-walking company, volunteered at Hospice and various animal rescues, coached kids in the Special Olympics, tended bar, made and sold jewelry, and even studied several forms of spiritual healing — but it wasn't until I began coaching youth roller hockey in El Segundo, California, that my path would soon change from one of lost and confused to one of deeper meaning and true love.

The unexpected and abrupt ending of my professional skating days was an overwhelming loss. I stayed in Florida a little longer, hoping to distract myself by spending time with friends and playing hockey. It didn't matter what I did, I still had an immeasurable emptiness inside that only seemed to be temporarily relieved by food. Not the healthy foods I eat most of the time, but the crap that I try to avoid. I have always struggled with moderation. It didn't matter whether it was drinking, gambling, truck or dog sizes — now it was with food.

I clearly remember the day when I finally called my mom to tell her I needed help. I had just come out of the corner market with a bag of food for a planned binge, and wondered how the guy at the cash register knew I was so distraught. I didn't realize, until I got back into my truck, that I had forgotten to clean off the mascara that was streaming down my cheeks from my most recent crying episode. I struggled through each day with the cold, hard realization that RollerJam would be no more. I felt completely lost.

I had gone from being a heartbroken eighteen-year-old with no real direction, to an overnight television success. Going back to what felt like a nobody was devasting. It left me yearning to have some control in my life in any area that I could, and that area became my body.

Prior to skating professionally, I never paid much attention to my physique. Sure, I hated my flat chest and used to think that if only I had boobs, Mark would have wanted to be with me. Outside of that, I didn't focus too much on my figure, or watch what I put into my mouth. I ate when I was hungry and stopped when I wasn't. Fame and spandex changed that. The more I learned about food and nutrition, the more it began taking over my life. I obsessively monitored every morsel I consumed while also tracking every calorie I burned though exercise. This process was exhausting, and it felt like a full-time job. Controlling my caloric input and calorie burning output was exactly that — *control*. It was the control I longed for and couldn't seem to find in any other way. And although my flat chest had also been out of my control, I took care of that with implants shortly before RollerJam.

Prior to undergoing cosmetic surgery, I felt like I looked masculine and unattractive without breasts, but I couldn't imagine taking the time off from hockey to consider having a procedure done.

The opportunity presented itself after the National Roller Hockey Championships when I severely shattered my arm. It was the first shift of our first game when it happened. I was taken by ambulance from the tournament in Vancouver, Canada, to a hospital in Seattle, Washington, to be treated. Word of advice; if you are ever going to get injured, do it in your own country. It was the longest ride imaginable. I was given the tiniest bag of self-administering morphine and a snarky suggestion to not use it too quickly because I wouldn't be allowed any more until we reached our destination. Seriously? *What in the actual fuck.*

The diagnosis was a spiral break in my upper arm, which damaged my radial nerve. The doctor said I'd be lucky to ever hold a hockey stick again. Those words didn't come easy to a someone who felt as if her entire life's purpose was to play that damn game. The recovery was grueling. My arm remained bundled and wrapped in a sling for months, with a very unusual looking device at the end of it. This "Edward Scissorhands" contraption allowed me to open and close my hand — something I couldn't do on my own due to my damaged nerve. People would gawk and whisper as they walked by, which made me feel defective. I was pissed off and hurt by their judgment, and often wondered what it must be like for people with true disabilities.

The healing process dragged on and I struggled with not knowing if I would ever be able to play hockey again. I didn't have much to look forward to until I began entertaining the idea of having my boobs done. The procedure was more painful than I had anticipated because the surgeon had to stretch my tight chest muscles in order to go from my non-existent AA cup into the full C's I had requested. Later, I was told I had the strongest chest muscles the doctor had ever seen — probably due to years of playing hockey.

My new boobs were still hiding behind their bandages, but I loved looking down and having something blocking my view for once. I was sure that the next time I ran into Mark, there would be no way he would be able to resist me, and I was right. We got back together, but my new physique didn't add anything to the longevity of the relationship. Mark broke my heart yet again, only a few months later, when he started seeing "Maggie" behind my back. In my opinion, Maggie wasn't even cute. How did I know? Because I showed up at Mark's door after a suspicious phone call from him canceling our plans, and there she was. Even though she wasn't what I would consider attractive, I desperately wanted to be her. I wanted to be the one inside Mark's house. I wanted to be the one he wanted.

CHAPTER NINE
ANXIETY AND ANTIDEPRESSANTS

If my new body wasn't good enough, what was? I spent too many years agonizing about Mark. I knew, without a doubt, he was the only one for me — thank God I was wrong. If only we could see things in the moment. When I look back at this door in my life closing — more like *slamming* — a much better door was opening for me; I just wasn't aware of it.

Have you ever experienced a heartbreak so difficult that you wondered how you would ever make it through? I'm learning that life is easier when I remind myself there is always something better coming. The more I trust this idea, the less I struggle when things don't seem to be working in my favor. Trusting that *somehow*, something really good will come out of my current situation helps to reduce any anxiety I have. Everything seems to improve rapidly when I am able to change my focus from how bad something is, to reminding myself that something good will come from this experience. I now recognize that I have greater influence over my life than what I previously thought.

I spent years feeling pressured to conform to society, rather than doing what seemed right inside. I didn't feel like it was acceptable to be unique, and instead of being celebrated and supported around my differences; I often found myself in trouble when I didn't succumb to societal norms. When we don't fit into society's one-size-fits-all box, we get a label: A.D.D., A.D.H.D., O.C.D., Dyslexic, Depressed. I was marked and medicated for all of the above. Sometimes medication is exactly what is needed, and sometimes it's given out like candy. I probably fell somewhere in between, and accepting myself for who I really am has been a journey.

Most of these so-called problems began showing up in my life during the years I was forced to visit my dad every other weekend. It was a visitation schedule mandated by the court, and I hated it. I'd spend the twelve days between visits dreading the next one. As soon as I would get to my dad's house, I would routinely ask if I could take Pepto Bismol. It wasn't until years later that I finally connected the uneasiness I used to feel in my stomach, to what was actually intense anxiety. I was always uncomfortable when I was there.

It was my dad's inability to stand up for me against my stepmom, Patricia, that left me feeling so unsafe. She wanted to paint a picture-perfect image of her family, which included her two children from a previous marriage. In her eyes, I didn't fit in. Patricia seemed to disapprove of everything about me. She was always appalled by my appearance. *"Your mom let you leave the house like that?"* she would question after seeing my mismatched clothing or unruly hair. It was obvious I didn't come close to her idea of perfection.

An example of being treated differently was how Patricia expected me to do things that weren't in my best interest. Frequently, she would encourage me to finish any leftovers that sat on the kitchen counter in her attempt to keep the area tidy, instead of just throwing the food away. I felt like a human garbage can. Generally, it was junk food that her own children were not allowed to eat, because she feared they would gain weight. God forbid her biological kids carried any extra meat on their bones. Perhaps this was what created the foundation for my future struggles with food.

During these dreaded visits, I rarely saw my dad, because he worked weekends. This meant I was usually stuck going to the mall with my stepfamily. The long hours spent shopping were never for my benefit. The intention was always the same; to find the trendiest shoes, fanciest designer jeans, and big-name labels for Patricia's children. I remember one trip in particular, when I spotted a cheap pair of plastic earrings I really liked. I begged Patricia to buy them for me, and to my surprise, she actually did! Those inexpensive earrings didn't come without a hefty price tag though; I was reminded constantly of how thankful I should be for her "gift."

One day, my dad and grandma joined us to shop at a local discount store, where I fell in love with a pair of tennis shoes; something I actually needed. My grandma jumped at the opportunity to buy them because it was rare that she shopped with us and she wanted to treat me to something. Patricia was outraged. She screamed at my dad and blamed him for my grandmother's kind offer, because in her mind, it was not okay for me to receive something while her kids didn't. *Are you kidding me? You've bought them new things every single visit since I've known you!* But of course, I didn't say that — I was just a kid without a voice. *Did my dad say anything?* Fuck no, he didn't.

The final straw that ended my forced visitation was when Patricia yanked me out of a donut store where I was waiting with my dad and threw me against some newspaper stands. She had become enraged and was screaming at me because my stepsister told her that I didn't love her. The episode was scary, humiliating, and completely erroneous — as I had never said such a thing; at least not out loud. God bless you in heaven dad, but your lack of balls when it came to standing up for me was fucked.

Even with his inability to parent, I loved my dad and fought endlessly for his attention. The focus of his entire life, though, was his "other" family, and making sure they were always happy and cared for. He only made the effort to see me when it was convenient for him; this made me feel unimportant.

Our fences began to mend in my late teens when Patricia and my dad showed up unexpectedly to attend the filming of RollerJam that was taking place in Las Vegas. Initially, I was pissed to learn she was there — after all, I hadn't had to face Patricia in nearly a decade. Once my anger subsided, I chose to confront her. That conversation was the beginning of clearing the rancid air that had kept us apart for years, and now I've come to really love and appreciate Patricia.

Since my dad's passing a few years ago, I have spent more time with my stepfamily than I ever did while he was here. Darcy has become one of my closest friends and she is often the first person I call when I need someone to talk to. Our pregnancies happened to coincide, and we spent a majority of that special (but sometimes awful) time together, mainly by phone, as she lives more than three hours from me.

Darcy's baby shower was four years ago, and my dad showed up unexpectedly at the end of the event to say hello. I was completely annoyed with him, knowing the only reason he stopped by was because the shower was close to his home and convenient for him. One thing that used to make me cringe whenever I saw my dad, was when he would expect me to kiss him each time we said hello or good-bye. It always disgusted me. As I left that day, I begrudgingly obliged him with a half-assed peck on his cheek and went about my way.

CHAPTER TEN
GOODBYE DAD

It was only a few days later, on Easter morning, when Patricia called me at an unusually early hour. My dad was in the hospital — and his heart was failing. *I don't understand. I had just seen him, and he was fine, wasn't he?* That's when she let me know he hadn't felt well for quite some time, but stubbornly wouldn't consider seeing a doctor. I quickly got dressed, drove several traffic-filled hours south from Calabasas to Anaheim and met my sister at the hospital. Together, we entered his room where he was swiftly being prepped for surgery. Even though things were a little chaotic and crowded, it felt important to let him know we were there.

Darcy and I, both feeling uneasy, stood on opposite sides of his bed. We each took one of his hands and placed them on our growing bellies, reminding him that he needed to get well and meet his grandbabies soon. Those words felt insufficient as they were spoken. Somehow, I knew this was the last time we would see him. As I leaned in to kiss his forehead before slipping quietly out of the room, I wondered if anyone else knew, too? Maybe the doctors did — I'll never know. I wasn't prepared for him to go when he did. We still had unfinished business to take care of. Sometimes I wish he could have met my children — but in reality, how often would he have actually seen them? Throughout my life, it was a struggle for us to have any quality time together. He was always on the road, always working, and always overly consumed with his "other" family.

On rare occasions, prior to my dad's passing, he would attempt to surprise me by asking if I was going to be home on such and such day. It was never because he was going to make the three-hour drive to see me — it was because Patricia had a doctor, dentist, or hair appointment near where I lived, and since it was *convenient,* he wanted to stop by. The hurt of not being a priority in his life was still there. I would tell him not to bother coming and to call me when seeing *me* was the actual point of the visit. I despised feeling like second fiddle.

Losing my dad was hard, but what was even harder was when I learned how my dad was actually a *real* father to my stepfamily; the type of dad I begged for years to have in my life. It was as if we experienced two entirely different people. My dad was the lying, unavailable, incapable one and my stepfamily got the fun, giving, loving, and thoughtful dad. I didn't know how true this was until I sat at his funeral, listening to his other family speak so highly of him at the podium. I was in complete shock as they sang praise after praise about what kind of a father my dad was; going out for ice cream, family boat rides, fun vacations… Surely, they couldn't possibly be talking about the man I called dad.

My stepdad, Steve, graciously attended the funeral to support me, and was pissed as he listened to the preposterous stories about my dad. Steve spent years witnessing my struggles and tried to help me navigate that dysfunctional, heartbreaking relationship I experienced. The ironic part about that closing chapter was that my dad always wanted us to all be together and *appear* as one big, happy family — and following his funeral, he got exactly that. We all went to lunch at one of his favorite restaurants, and lovingly sat around the table reminiscing. It felt like he was around us, shaking his head as if to say, "It's about time!" One of my dad's few positive traits was being a jokester — it was something I appreciated about him. I chose to honor him by giving my son his middle name, James. Oh crap, my dad's middle name is actually *Jeffrey*. It was Titan who had the middle name, James. I named my first born after my dog. Sorry, dad. I guess *that* joke is on you.

CHAPTER ELEVEN
MY BIGGEST CRITIC

Landon James was born three months after my dad's passing and was followed by his sister, Lexi Jo, twenty-one months later. I love my children more than anything in the world, and yet my drive for accomplishment sometimes makes me feel like I have a war going on inside. I'm continually searching for a balance between motherhood and career — if there is such a thing. I just wish I could sit still long enough to enjoy crafting, snacking, building, and baking with them; the way I imagine other mothers do.

I scramble to keep up with the slew of professions that being a mom includes; housekeeper, teacher, chef, laundress, bill payer, finance organizer, doctor, project manager, schedule keeper, appointment maker, taxi driver, dog walker ... you get the point.

However, the most important role for me currently, is to model authenticity for my kids. In the past, I put a lot of energy into appearing as though I had my shit together. Upholding my façade was difficult to maintain. Showing up as real, open and — gasp —vulnerable as I can these days, has its own challenges. It's even more difficult when I'm around others who are pretending to have a flawless life. I get it. I spent years living this way.

Practicing authenticity means saying what's on my mind even though I may be judged for it. An example of this is admitting that I'm feeling anything less than blessed when talking about raising kids. I used to censor everything I said and I set impossible standards for myself. I spent so much time critiquing my lumpy thighs and caring too much about what other people thought. I made my life much harder than it needed to be. Maybe everyone does this to themselves at some point or another. If they do, they don't seem to talk about it. I suppose it is all a little embarrassing — but in reality, who's looking at my thighs, anyway?

The height of my self-criticism was in middle school. My mom's boyfriend at the time, Richard, often teased me by saying: "*A moment on the lips, forever on the hips.*" Usually this comment came just before I was about to eat something delicious. Something meant to be savored. *Thanks, asshole.* It's pretty hard to enjoy something when you are eleven-years-old and constantly aware of your awkwardly growing, prepubescent body. Between my dad's lack of praise and Richard's constant criticism, it's no wonder my self-worth plummeted.

It was more than just my changing figure that Richard provoked me to feel bad about. "*Nice body, shame about your face*" was another of his overused attempts at poking fun. Looking back, his behavior was appalling. I'm shocked my mom would let this go on, but maybe she wasn't even aware of it. Perhaps I am recalling this in a different way than it was said? Maybe it was somehow done in a loving manner? Whatever it was, it stuck, as I can still feel the sting of it thirty years later.

Compounding the difficulty of my middle school years came as a result of a freak accident on a friend's trampoline. A doctor's visit led to the discovery of my severely curved spine, shattering my confidence in an entirely different way. My spine was so twisted that I was left with only two options: I could have surgery — in which they would fuse my spine and place steel rods along my spinal column — or I could try wearing a hideous brace twenty-three hours a day for two years. I think the only reason I opted for the brace was because I was an avid figure skater at the time and knew that having metal objects in my back wouldn't allow my body to bend in the ways it needed in order to perform.

The brace was awful. It was constructed of thick plastic and Velcro and went around my entire torso from my hipbones to my armpits. This new contraption was a huge embarrassment, and I was desperate to find a way to hide it from the kids at school. My mom was always pretty creative and thought that if I could somehow hide the brace *under* my shirts, instead of on top, it wouldn't be as easily noticed — as long as my shirts were on the baggy side. The idea was great, until we realized that if I leaned forward in the slightest, it would cause the top of the brace to make a very obvious "ridge" across my back from shoulder to shoulder. That's when we came up with Plan B: Buy two of every shirt and use one to make a hood to sew onto the other shirt. Basically, all of my shirts would become "hoodies." This idea was *awesome,* and it worked perfectly for weeks, until a boy on the school bus came up and tapped me on the back. He loudly exclaimed, after feeling something foreign, *"What the heck is under your shirt?" Is that plastic?"* He kept questioning me while simultaneously knocking his fists on my body. The entire bus quickly became curious too, and kids began to call me a freak. If only it had stopped there. It wasn't long before everyone at school knew about my brace, and the next two years of junior high were nothing short of agonizing.

Another source of embarrassment was my big, Jewish nose. Yeah, one of the perks of being Jewish is the often gigantic schnozzle that comes with it. Speaking of religion, even though both of my parents were Jewish, we celebrated both Hanukkah *and* Christmas. By the time I was ten, it was just Christmas. I joke about being a really bad Jew, as I most certainly can't tell you when Passover is or what it represents. My Catholic-raised husband likes to poke fun, and usually lets me know when the first night of Hanukkah comes around every year. I admit there is one Jewish tradition that I do enjoy; gefilte fish. Gross, I know.

So, this nose of mine — it was huge — like *really* huge. From the front it didn't look too bad, but from the side? My God! I used to be mortified at the thought of someone seeing my profile. So much so, that I would carry around a tissue to hold up to the side of my face in a desperate attempt to hide my unsightly "beak" from the world. I did this for years — that's how embarrassed I felt by it. The ridicule from classmates was just brutal. Kids can be such assholes! I was sure that if only my nose were normal, I would be pretty, and therefore happy. When I was fourteen, my mom scheduled a consultation for me with a well-known plastic surgeon. I think it must have broken her heart to know how bullied and tormented I was every day. Finally, it happened — I had a *new nose!* Even with all of the tape and dried blood that had pooled beneath my nostrils, I remember going to a nearby shopping mall the day after surgery and feeling so confident! I didn't care if people thought I had a nose job, a broken nose, or some kind of sinus surgery — because it was smaller, *much smaller*, and that's the only thing in my life that seemed to really matter at the time.

When it was time to start high school, I had high hopes that things would be different. After all, I was going to have a fresh start; the brace was gone, I was at a new school, and had a new nose. By this time,

I had become fully immersed and was excelling in hockey, which gave me a newfound confidence in myself. As it turned out, high school freshmen are just as cruel as middle school kids. The bullying and peer pressure continued. I dreaded going to school every day and usually came home in tears.

The days crept along and several months later, an opportunity to study at home presented itself. I think my mom struggled with the decision to homeschool for a long time; wondering if she made the right choice. I really appreciated this option as it allowed me the freedom to be myself in my own environment. I thrived in home study. I was in charge of my own schedule, held myself accountable to get the assignments done and graduated a few years later with nearly straight A's.

CHAPTER TWELVE
BREAKING FREE

My healing process didn't fully begin until I hit bottom after RollerJam ended. I finally reached out for help with my struggles surrounding food, and I checked in to an inpatient treatment center — even though I was scared shitless. I wondered what I would do there. What would it be like? Was it going to be like what I have seen in movies? Would the patients all be insane? I certainly wasn't insane — I just didn't always make the best choices when food was involved. Who was I kidding; food was ruling my life. How would someone be able to fix that for me? But the thing that made me the most nervous was that someone at the facility might recognize me from TV.

My new daily routine felt like a cross between being treated like a child and a prisoner. The rules were strict and everything needed to be done in an exact way. My only contact with the outside world was through letter writing and a pay phone. With only a single phone call allowed each day, I wondered why they didn't make us wear black and white stripes. Prison likeness aside, the program was helpful; at least while I was in attendance. However, it wasn't long after completion that I had my first "slip-up." Before I knew it, I was back to where I started — only this time I knew better, but I couldn't snap myself out if it. Bingeing after completing treatment felt much worse than it had prior, and from there I continued down the slippery slope of disordered eating — until I finally began to deal with my true inner feelings.

I've come a long way since then. Are my thoughts surrounding food and my body as gentle as I'd like them to be? No. But when I get caught up in striving for perfection, I remind myself that trying to be perfect is exhausting.

During times that my self-esteem was at its lowest, even the *thought* of not wearing makeup used to make me uneasy. God forbid someone would catch a glimpse of my bare skin, huge pores, acne scars, and rosacea in all of their glory. Would they see what I saw when I looked in the mirror? Maybe they would be too focused on my bumpy thighs instead. These thoughts used to consume me when I lacked approval of myself.

My journey from critical self-judgment to a more balanced emotional state was imperceptible at first.

My focus seemed to revolve around how mistreated, unworthy, and unloved I felt. This had become my life's "story," and I was oblivious to the consequences that came with this negative way of thinking. It was like digging a deeper hole for myself and just making things worse.

For a majority of my life, I was in and out of conventional therapy, and while I did find aspects of it helpful, I discovered other opportunities that gave me a better roadmap out of my personal hell. The biggest changes came when I finally took charge of my thinking. My thoughts used to be focused on what *had been*, instead of accepting "what is." I stopped fighting my past, and began making peace with it. Now I am able to see how my early struggles have turned into strengths through my improved self-worth, strong determination, the ability to speak my truth and stand up for myself. The combination of a difficult beginning — and the climb out of it — has helped to shape me into the healthier person I am today. The small adjustments in some of my negative thinking had a huge influence on the direction my life began to go — including no longer attracting the unhealthy relationships I had been choosing.

When my husband entered my life, it was the first time I wasn't seeking the hard-to-get, bad-boy type. I always sought emotionally unavailable men, and then spent so much time consumed by my romantic status, or lack thereof. When I was alone, I was pining for someone and when I had someone, I lived in fear they would leave me.

That conflict no longer exists. I feel safe with Jason. He has supported me when I have felt like it was me against the world, and he has talked me through some of my darkest times. Jay is my biggest cheerleader and I trust that he is not going anywhere. The steadiness of my marriage allows me to focus on my goals and dreams, something I had not experienced in previous relationships.

CHAPTER THIRTEEN
RISING ABOVE

I have come to realize the importance of stability in childhood. I want to create a strong foundation for my children so they are emotionally secure and able to follow their passions, rather than having to navigate through unnecessary turmoil — as I did.

Think about the expectations we have set for our kids. Are we measuring them against society's idea of what is "normal" even though comparison may be detrimental to them? How might this affect their self-worth? Are we strengthening their self-esteem or weakening it?

I am often in awe over my children's abilities to live in the moment. I watch as they fill with pride each time they complete something simple. What happens to that natural inner satisfaction over time? What changes inside of us? Does it start in early education — when a child's ideas may not match that of their teacher — and so they "fail?" Is this when we start to fall into the mold of the population and no longer feel as free to express who we really are? Is this when conformity begins? Whose right is it, besides our own, to decide how we are to be in the world?

Many of us set unattainable standards for ourselves and in turn feel "less than" when we don't achieve what we set out to accomplish. Whose ideals are we trying to live up to? Are we driven by our own desire for improvement, or are we being influenced by what we think others expect from us? No wonder we often fall short of our goals; they were never *our* goals to begin with.

I think it is important to question the norm and what society considers "acceptable." Each one of us is so uniquely different that it seems wrong to be expected to do things in the same way. While some kids will thrive in a traditional school setting, some won't — but should they really be punished for their different needs? They are, I was, and it isn't okay.

While one of my children will probably do just fine fitting into the expectations of our current educational system, my other child has a much better chance of thriving by doing things differently.

I don't expect society to change for my children. My role as a parent is to reach for the opportunities that will be the best match for each of my kids. It is also my job to turn away from comparison to other families and ignore the external pressure to raise my children in a way that isn't in their best interest. My obligation is to support them in becoming emotionally balanced individuals with healthy self-esteem and a passion for learning; whatever that may look like.

Between the influence of one's role models and archaic educational expectations, of course kids are easily swayed. When I was younger and heavily shamed about my thighs, you can imagine what I obsessively thought about for the next two decades. What if my mom's boyfriend Richard had chosen to comment on how strong my legs were, instead of criticizing them? Words are immensely powerful.

I spent more than half of my life trying to squeeze into ridiculous expectations so that I would feel accepted. This is not something I want to pass down. Maybe you have also felt the pull toward perfection and the pressure to fit into a mold that society dictates as acceptable. Or perhaps you, too, are raising young children and long for them not to experience any unneeded struggles, as you did. Explore other options, set aside any possible judgment from others. It is easy to be consumed with the idea that life needs to be lived within predetermined parameters — but who set those guidelines and did they have our own unique character and abilities in mind?

Try not to let others' opinions pressure you into doing the 'wrong' thing for your child, especially when you can clearly see that something different is needed for their well-being.

Don't get sucked into the artificial portrayals of perfection that contaminate our world, prompting us all to wonder: *Am I really enough?*

Me with my mom and dad

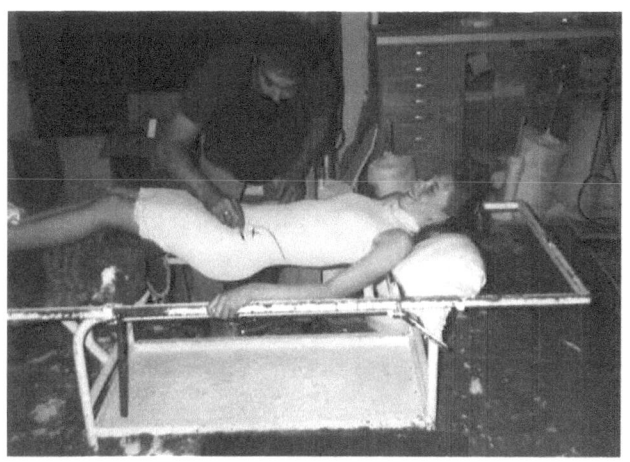

Casting a brace for my scoliosis

The cast and contraption that allowed me to use my hand

Leader of the pack Laura Weintraub of the Nevada Hot Dice brings beauty, muscle and power to the banked track on the new season of ROLLERJAM. TNN's action-packed, popular series returns for a second season on <u>Friday, Aug. 27</u> (9:00-11:00 PM, ET/PT).

Dancing with my dad at my stepsister's wedding

www.ingramcontent.com/pod-product-compliance
Lightning Source LLC
Chambersburg PA
CBHW030309100526
44590CB00012B/578